Guide to Government Grants Writing

Guide to Government Grants Writing

✦

Tools for Success

Harriet Grayson, M.U.P., M.A.
Focus Fundraising

iUniverse, Inc.
New York Lincoln Shanghai

Guide to Government Grants Writing
Tools for Success

iUniverse books may be ordered through booksellers or by contacting:

iUniverse
2021 Pine Lake Road, Suite 100
Lincoln, NE 68512
www.iuniverse.com
1-800-Authors (1-800-288-4677)

ISBN-13: 978-0-595-37785-5 (pbk)
ISBN-13: 978-0-595-82159-4 (ebk)
ISBN-10: 0-595-37785-8 (pbk)
ISBN-10: 0-595-82159-6 (ebk)

Printed in the United States of America

Contents

CHAPTER 1   Learning the System 1

CHAPTER 2   State Government Funding—Grants &
Contracts. 11

CHAPTER 3   Key Elements Enhance Success 17

CHAPTER 4   Judging the Future Based on Past Performance 21

CHAPTER 5   What's The Problem? 25

CHAPTER 6   The Body of the Grant Application 29

CHAPTER 7   Writing the Budget 34

CHAPTER 8   Rejection 40

CHAPTER 9   Individuals need to be Creative 42

CHAPTER 10   Small Towns and Cities. 47

CHAPTER 11   In Conclusion 52

1

Learning the System

♦

It matters what level of government funding is being sought

You may already know that the United States government has billions of dollars to distribute in the form of grants to contractors. You probably just don't know how to get your share of it. The purpose of this manual is to assist all types of organizations—nonprofits, small cities and towns, faith-based groups, for-profit businesses as well as individuals to successfully receive government grant funding. Most of these funds are available through an open competition process, which is increasingly being announced to the public by the different government agencies through the Internet. The federal government has become a major supporter of the use of this new technology. In fact, most application forms can be completed on line.

Government funding is linked to budget cycles usually reflecting the fiscal accounting cycle of the originating agency. For example, the federal fiscal year begins October 1st, therefore many federal funding application deadlines, as well as the release of funding are tied to that fiscal cycle. A grant application referring to federal FY2006 means that the funding cycle begins October 1, 2005 and ends September 30, 2006. State governments operate on a different fiscal cycle; likewise grants are more likely to be announced and rewarded based on the state cycles. All but four states run their fiscal years from July 1 to June 30. The four exceptions are: New York State and Texas which run their fiscal cycles from April 1 through March 31st, and Alabama and Michigan operate their fiscal cycles identical to the federal fiscal cycle, October 1 through September 30th.

In recent years, it has become more common that applications can receive favorable reviews, yet not be funded. There are two factors responsible for this reality—shrinking government budgets and political delays in government budgets being approved by the appropriate legislative body. The result is an organization may indeed be sent an award letter and then later another letter indicating that the application would have been funded had additional funds been available. **A suggestion—never hire or enter into a subcontract based on a favorable review or receipt of an award letter unless the organization actually receives a signed contract from the originating government agency.**

RFP—RFA

A RFP (Request for Proposal) or RFA (Request for Application) are the most commonly found grant opportunity announcements. However, government agencies do use other terms. For example, the federal Department of Justice requests "Solicitations" while the federal Environmental Protection Agency may announce RFIP (Request for Initial Grant Proposals) because many of their initial announcements are used as screening devices. An organization submits a first application and a majority of those applications are rejected. Those remaining applicants then submit a more detailed application for the actual funding. State agencies may simply refer to a grant opportunity as a PA (Public Announcement).

There are good internet sites to look at for grant announcements, but there is no one site that lists them all. The federal government has become more technologically sophisticated in recent years so that a variety of RFPs or RFAs can be located on the major federal grant site—www.grants.gov. The Centers for Disease Control and Prevention (CDC) announced in May 2005 that their entire grant funding opportunity announcements will be available through www.grants.gov. Unfortunately, not all RFPs or RFAs are registered on that site. Also, most states are not as organized so there are a myriad of sites for locating state and local funding.

In addition, state and local governments use newspapers to make grant announcements. Scrutinize the larger circulation newspapers in your community under the "Public Notices" section for RFPs.

Individuals seeking government funding need to look beyond the RFP or RFA sites. Individuals should search for grant opportunities using the descriptors Scholarship, Fellowship, or Internship because these indicate government programs specifically designed for individuals. The majority of individual grants are in the form of awards usually to scholars, researchers, teachers or artists. Specific strategies for individuals seeking government funding will be discussed in a separate chapter.

Federal Government

The largest funding source in the United States is the federal government. The majority of grant opportunities are awarded to organizations that have previously received federal funding. However, the federal government is always seeking to expand its list of grantees, if for no other reason than it looks better politically. In fact, the federal government has created special categories of awards directed to new entrants such as "Seed Money" grants, and those for organizations with small budgets (under $300,000) and those in existence for fewer than three years. It is unlikely for a brand new organization (under one year) to receive federal funding because an important element in a successful award is demonstrated fiscal responsibility. The federal government determines this by reviewing an organization's audited financial statements.

All organizations should start reviewing federal funding opportunities by clicking on the federal Web site www.grants.gov. Twenty-six federal agencies are listed on this site representing over 900 different grant programs and more than $350 billion in annual awards. The number of agencies participating will increase over time since the goal of the federal Office of Management and Budget is to centralize and computerize the grant application process. As of 2005, some of the largest federal agencies are represented on this site including: Department of Agriculture, Commerce, Defense, Education, Health & Human Services, Housing & Urban Development, Justice, Labor, Transportation, National Science Foundation and FEMA. However, one should never assume this site has all grant opportunities listed, so it is always advisable to also directly search the Web site of specific federal agencies such as Health and Human Services (HHS) or Housing and Urban Development (HUD). These are very large federal agencies with multiple levels of agencies under these behemoths. It is equally important to search out grants directly announced by sub-agencies. For example, HHS is the largest federal agency and is the parent of big and important grantor agencies such as the Administration for Children and Families (ACF), Administration on Aging (AoA), Food and Drug Administration (FDA), National Institutes of Health (NIH) and Centers for Disease Control and Prevention (CDC) as well as the Office for Public Health Emergency Preparedness and Center for Faith-Based and Community Initiatives. Determine the agencies most likely to offer grant opportunities that fit your organization and then constantly monitor those sites.

The next important step in successfully obtaining government funding is to better understand the federal granting bureaucracy by seeking out your organization's Congressional representative. Locate the office of your representative and contact staff in that district office. If your organization is unknown to the district office staff, invite them to your offices and let them see or learn about what contribution your organization is making to the community. Ask the Congressional staff in the district office if they have suggestions of contact people in federal agencies and specific internet sites to utilize regarding grant opportunities. Increasingly, your federal representatives are creating electronic ways to reach their constituents, most commonly by creating e-mail newsletters. In some cases, theses newsletters announce grant opportunities. Be sure to sign up for all available newsletters.

Getting Started

While the federal application process appears daunting, it is largely the completion of a series of forms followed by the creation of a project narrative and the development of a budget with a budget justification. Almost all federal applications start with Standard Form 424 (Rev. 9-2003)—Application for Federal Assistance. Periodically, the forms are revised so be sure to complete the latest version. Review the on-line application to quickly learn the latest version.

In order to complete this form, your organization has to have accomplished several other steps along the way. First, your organization needs an Employer Identification Number (EIN) assigned by the Internal Revenue Service. Second, your organization needs a DUNS identification number or Data Universal Number System provided by the commercial credit rating company Duns and Bradstreet (D & B). This is a recent requirement. It's easy to obtain. Call 1-866-705-5711 or register on-line. The Form 424 also requires listing the Congressional District of the applicant as well as where the project is located. Usually a grant announcement has a title and an accompanying Catalog of Federal Domestic Assistance Number (CFDA). You must include this number on the Form 424. Also, the Form 424 requests a geographic description of where the project will be located—city, county, state, etc. As part of the documentation for any government grant application it's always advisable to include demographics and if possible, a map delineating the physical geography of the project.

Local/state governments need to check whether an application is subject to review by State Executive Order 12372 through the State Single Point of Contact (SPOC) to determine whether the application is subject to intergovernmental review.

Other Forms

The federal government wants assurances that your organization follows the restrictions, regulations and laws that have been enacted. Standard Form 424B is the "Assurances—Non-Construction Programs." This form is an all-in-one legal promise that your organization can fulfill all the requirements of the particular grant you are seeking. It demands that the organization comply with all Federal statues regarding nondiscrimination. The language of Form 424B speaks to federal laws such as Title VI of the Civil Rights Act of 1964, Title IX of the Education Amendments of 1972, Section 504 of the Rehabilitation Act of 1973, Age Discrimination Act of 1975, Drug Abuse Office and Treatment Act of 1972, Comprehensive Alcohol Abuse and Alcoholism Prevention, Treatment and Rehabilitation Act of 1970. This language is standard legalese and should not present any problems; however, if your organization has been cited for discrimination, then you should consult your attorney and review carefully the language of these assurances.

Other issues addressed in Form 424B include compliance with the federal Hatch Act limiting political activities of employees: Davis-Bacon Act sets labor standards, environmental standards under a series of federal laws and the catch-all phrase: "Will comply with all applicable requirements of all other Federal laws, executive orders, regulations and policies governing this program." Unless your organization has been cited for violations under federal law, the only important assurance that you must be prepared to accept is the organization's willingness to meet required financial and compliance audits in accordance with the Single Audit Act of 1984. In other words, be prepared, and expect to be audited by the federal government.

The "Certifications" Sheet is similar to Form 424B. It contains language concerning five certifications or what can be referred to as declarations. "Certification 1" refers to debarment and suspension. This certification asks has the organization been debarred, suspended, declared ineligible for federal funding because of fraud or some other criminal act. "Certification 2" deals with maintaining a drug-free workplace. "Certification 3" concerns the prohibition against lobbying. "Certification 4" certifies that all the statements given are true, complete and accurate. "Certification 5" refers to maintaining a smoke free environment.

The issue of lobbying is important for the federal government. In addition to the Certifications Form there is a specific form called the "Disclosure of Lobbying Activities" which must be completed.

A private, non-profit organization must be prepared to demonstrate evidence of their nonprofit status. The easiest proof is to provide a copy of a valid Internal Revenue Service 501c(3) Letter of Determination.

Applying On-Line

The government application process has joined the twentieth-first century permitting a number of federal agencies to accept grant applications electronically. However, there is a registration process that must be followed. Again, these are not difficult steps, but it does demand thinking ahead of the deadline. The on-line system is accessed by visiting www.grants.gov.

The on-line system requires an applicant to register with the Central Contractor Registry (CCR). In doing so, the organization designates an E-Business Point of Contact (EPOC). This is an important selection for the organization so choose the individual wisely. It is the EPOC who is authorized to designate or revoke an individual's ability to submit grant applications on behalf of their organization via grants.gov. A Director of Development who is a member of the organization's senior ranks is a possible choice. A small organization may consider a senior level financial officer. The CCR also contains basic information about the organization minimizing the need to re-enter this information on a subsequent e-grant application.

The next step is to Register with Credential Provider. This step is important to safeguard the security of electronic information. Credential Providers authenticates the parties authorized to submit applications. The Credential Provider for grants.gov is Operational Research Consultants (ORC). By registering with ORC an organization receives a username and password making that individual the Authorized Organization Representative (AOR). Once the person is registered the EPOC is asked to validate the registration. After this happens, the AOR will receive notification via email confirming they are authorized to submit grant applications through grants.gov.

This may seem like a cumbersome process but it is really very useful if your organization intends to apply for multiple grants with agencies that are listed. Eventually, all federal agencies will be on this system. There is on-line assistance ("Customer Support") and a tutorial to help you get started. If your organization writes one federal grant a year then this process may be more troublesome than useful.

State Government

Although the federal government awards the greatest number of grants and usually the largest monetary awards, organizations are more likely to receive direct funding from their state government. The federal government makes significant awards directly to state government agencies. As a result, organizations residing in states where state government agencies are the most aggressive about getting funding from the federal government are more likely to obtain funding. Some federal government funding to states is based solely on population; therefore, the most populous states receive the most funding. In addition, certain federal monies are targeted to states with high levels of poverty, therefore organizations in these states are more likely to receive funding for programs targeting the poor and disadvantaged.

As organized as the federal government has become in creating electronic services and easy researching tools, states are far behind in this modernization process. It is tricky and difficult to quickly locate grant opportunities offered by states. Some state agencies are better equipped than others. The first step is simply to proceed to your state's official home page on the Web. Chapter 2 discusses the nuances of state government funding.

County Government

Across the country, large counties receive direct funding from both the federal and state government for most programs. In turn, the county governments make funds available through RFPs or RFA' to other organizations and individuals. Each county operates in its own distinct style and using its own procedures. The best advice is to locate the official county web page and check the announcements every two weeks. The process of securing county government grant funds is highly variable; however, it is easier to establish relationships with county agency officials so it's important to find contacts at county agencies.

City Government

Large cities do make funding available that they receive from state and federal sources. It can be difficult to break into these systems because of long-established relationships especially if the political officials have been in power for many years.

One source for general information on cities is www.statelocalgov.net. Depending on how much data is provided by the sources, it may start as the first step in an investigation of possible competitive RFPs.

One city-centered organization that does provide funding for programs is the National League of Cities (www.nlc.org). This is a good source to consult about potential grant opportunities.

Eligibility

This is the first issue to be addressed by a potential applicant. Am I eligible? This should be a very easy question to ascertain. The Federal Register has a specific item on its announcements. The "Eligible Applicants" section lists who can apply; however, an organization may have to check with another government body to confirm its eligibility. For example, in a recent RFP by the federal Department of Education, eligible applicants are listed as "a foundation, museum, library, for-profit business, public or private nonprofit organization or community-based organization including faith-based organizations…a local educational agency (LEA) including a charter school that meets its State's definition of an LEA." Before a charter school submits an application it will need to know whether it meets its State's definition of an LEA. Sometimes the definition of eligibility is multi-layered. For example, a recent state of New York Education Department RFP stated, "In order to be eligible to apply for these grants, an organization must be a consumer controlled, not-for-profit 501c(3) with a governing board that is comprised of fifty percent or more people with disabilities. The governing board must be the principal policy setting body of the organization." Before moving forward on this grant opportunity, an organization either has such a board in place or can quickly establish a board with these specific requirements. There is no point in submitting an application if your organization is ineligible.

Certain RFPs are released for specific geographical regions. The federal government has ten regions and RPF's are announced that cover only specified regions, sometimes only a specific state is mentioned so only potential awardees located in these geographic areas should apply. Carefully read any announcements to ascertain if there are geographic limitations.

Location matters in other ways. Certain federal grants such as those awarded by the Office of Justice, (US Department of Justice) pre-determine locations where the funding can be awarded based on crime statistics or where "pilot" or "seed" programs have already received initial funding. In a similar way, certain health grants are awarded to locations where there is a high incidence of certain health problems. So before embarking on an elaborate plan for completing an application, check these other factors. Does your organization's project reflect these required statistics?

In RFPs that have a research element there may be other eligibility requirements. For example, federal research grants require that the applicant's principal investigator(s) demonstrate the necessary research and academic credentials. To successful compete for this funding, the application must clearly show this fact, usually with a carefully constructed resume or curriculum vitae (c.v.). If the application requires a specific type of training; for example, completion of a course by the Centers for Disease Control (CDC) then the resume must reflect this training.

The government also emphasizes collaborations. Part of an eligibility clause in the RFP may be a statement about demonstrating the existence of a board, partnership, memorandum of agreement between groups. If this collaboration doesn't exist or cannot be created in time for the submission, then don't attempt to submit an application.

Letter of Intent (LOI)

In the RFP announcement, there can be a statement about submitting a Letter of Intent (LOI) prior to filing an application. This is not a binding obligation by an applicant. However, some agencies use the LOI to determine whether the project is even interesting enough for them to see the actual application. The grantor agency may use the LOI as a way of culling through many potential applicants. In some cases, the LOI is nothing more than a statement that the organization is interested in the RFP.

Review the requirements concerning the LOI carefully. It may state that without submitting an LOI, an organization is prohibited from later filing an application. In other cases, there is no requirement at all.

Usually a LOI is a small document, only one or two pages. If the requirement is that the LOI be no more than one-page then be sure to submit only one page. Follow the instructions. It is always advisable even if there is no requirement to file a LOI, do so anyway. It usually doesn't take too much time and it immediately puts your organization on the agency's mailing list so that any changes to the RFP or modifications will be sent to your organization.

Deadlines are Crucial

The above statement cannot be emphasized enough—deadlines are crucial. Observe not only the day a grant application is due but also the time of the day. Deadline times can be listed as end of the business day—you need to find out what time that is. More commonly a specific time will be on the RFP. Typically these times are either 4 or 5 PM, but they can be noon.

Letters of Intent have deadlines which must be respected. Forwarding backup documentation is sometimes required on a RFP. These requirements can have different deadlines but usually the timetable is within 30 days.

2

State Government
Funding—Grants & Contracts

◆

State Nuances

State government is one of the most important sources of funding for organizations of all kinds, including for-profit businesses. State governments also make funding available to individuals. There are two ways to view state funding opportunities. First, states issue RFAs and RFPs soliciting grant applications in a fashion similar to what the federal government does. In fact, an organization is more likely to receive funding from a state agency than the federal government. Much of the money that flows to state governments is directly from the federal government for the purpose of distributing the money to local entities. This means that all the intricate financial accounting required when obtaining direct federal government money remains the same in accepting state money.

Second, state governments offer extensive contracting and bidding opportunities that are available to organizations of all kinds and sometimes even individuals can directly bid for contracts. This is a neglected source of potential revenue. Nonprofit organizations should actively seek to learn more about the contract and bidding opportunities in the states where they operate. Organizations think of government contracting opportunities as paving roads and repairing bridges but bids are 'let' for services such as conducting surveys, providing after school tutoring, engineering reviews, etc. As more state and local governments decide to privatize traditional government services, new opportunities have arisen for outside organizations and sometimes for individuals to compete for contracts.

The states have yet to match the ease of using the federal on-line sites. There is no comprehensive grant site such as www.grants.gov on the state level. During the next several years, we anticipate greater sophistication on the part of states.

The first step is for an organization or individual to familiarize themselves with the official state web site. If there is a state agency that is of particular interest to your organization it behooves someone to check the state agency site(s) weekly for potential grant funding opportunities. Also check the state Web sites for bidding and contracting opportunities, which are also announced on-line.

State Web Sites

To simplify researching for state funding, a complete alphabetical listing of the 50 states is below. Careful review the available information on state Web sites. To begin the grant searching process start by identifying from the state site a listing of the different state agencies. Sometimes this process is cumbersome because it's not readily apparent how to obtain such a listing. Print or bookmark on your computer the site with the listing of state agencies. Then pinpoint those state agencies most likely to be sources of potential grant opportunities.

STATE	OFFICIAL STATE WEB SITE
Alabama	www.state.al.us
Alaska	www.state.ak.us
Arizona	az.gov/webapp/portal
Arkansas	www.arkansas.gov
California	www.ca.gov
Colorado	www.colorado.gov
Connecticut	www.ct.gov
Delaware	www.delaware.gov
Florida	www.myflorida.com
Georgia	www.georgia.gov
Hawaii	www.hawaii.gov
Idaho	www.state.id.us
Illinois	www.illinois.gov
Indiana	www.state.in.us
Iowa	www.iowa.gov
Kansas	www.state.ks.us

STATE	OFFICIAL STATE WEB SITE
Kentucky	www.kentucky.gov
Louisiana	www.louisiana.gov
Maine	www.state.me.us
Maryland	www.maryland.gov
Massachusetts	www.mass.gov
Michigan	www.michigan.gov
Minnesota	www.state.mn.us
Mississippi	www.state.mo.us
Montana	www.state.mt.us
Nebraska	www.nebraska.gov
Nevada	www.nv.gov
New Hampshire	www.state.nh.us
New Jersey	www.state.nj.us
New Mexico	www.state.nm.us
New York	www.state.ny.us
North Carolina	www.ncgov.com
North Dakota	discovernd.com
Ohio	www.ohio.gov
Oklahoma	www.ok.gov
Oregon	www.oregon.gov
Pennsylvania	www.state.pa.us
Rhode Island	www.ri.gov
South Carolina	www.discoversouthcarolina.com
South Dakota	www.state.sd.us
Tennessee	www.state.tn.us
Texas	www.state.tx.us
Utah	www.utah.gov

STATE	OFFICIAL STATE WEB SITE
Vermont	Vermont.gov
Virginia	www.virginia.gov
Washington	access.wa.gov
West Virginia	www.wv.gov
Wisconsin	www.wisconsin.gov
Wyoming	Wyoming.gov

State Differences

Every state's official Web site is going to be different reflecting the state's priorities or sometimes the Web site designer's interests. Small states such as Rhode Island and Kentucky have very elaborate and detailed state agency information on their state Web sites. Others states such as Tennessee and Vermont have sparse sites.

When researching potential opportunities, select the two or three state agencies which closely align themselves with the products or services your organization offers. Individuals should conduct a similar search. In rare cases, grant opportunities will be highlighted on the initial official state site. In most cases, if you search a specific state agency, available grant opportunities will be highlighted. If you have trouble navigating through a state's web site please let the webmasters know about your difficulties. State agencies want to make things easier so send an e-mail with your comments. Check nearby states for opportunities unless your organization or as an individual your licensing prohibits doing work in another state. Also it's recommended that grant researchers check all potential sources of funding beyond state agencies and include state commissions, quasi-public agencies such as housing authorities. Hidden in information about these authorities and commissions are funding opportunities.

Bidding Opportunities

Look beyond grant opportunities. Most state official sites also list 'bids and contract opportunities'. There are a variety of ways to identify these potential revenue sources. In some cases, the gateway to investigating these opportunities is easy to identify because it is clearly labeled 'Bid or Contract'. But also examine other labels such as 'How to do Business with State Government' or through a state Economic Development site. The sites for potential revenue are different than a site directing how to start or expand a business in a state. Initially, be prepared to spend a few hours navigating all potential routes to information.

Once you have identified the correct Web site most will encourage the organization or individual to register as a vendor. Do so even if you're not entirely certain about it. Then be sure to register for any and all e-mail announcements and newsletters.

Some state Web sites are extremely user friendly. The sites prominently list procurement opportunities. Outstanding examples are Connecticut and Indiana. Not all state official sites provide any simple way of accessing information about contracting opportunities. The following are states where contracting and bidding opportunities are notably displayed. Follow the specific steps indicated by clicking your computer mouse.

- Connecticut's state site calls attention to these offering with the title 'State Procurement Opportunities' on the official Web site
- Georgia uses the title 'State Purchasing' which leads to the site 'Bid Opportunities'
- Idaho's 'Government Contract and Purchasing' site leads to 'Vendor Information Bidding Opportunities'
- Indiana's official Web site has a 'Biz.In.gov Business Opportunities' site
- Louisiana lists the site 'Announcement and Notification' which leads to the 'Office of Contractual Review'—At this point you can subscribe and be made aware of pending opportunities
- Maryland register with 'eMaryland M@rketplace' as a vendor
- Massachusetts offers the opportunity to register as a potential contractor through the state official site which leads to 'Bids and Contracts'
- Minnesota has a featured site 'Solicitation Announcements'
- Montana uses the site 'Doing Business' which leads to 'State Bids and Proposals'
- North Carolina has a well developed vendor site start with 'NC E-Procurement@ Your Service'—register as a vendor under 'Vendor Registration'
- North Dakota's state site lists 'Vendor Registration' and then 'State Procurement Office'

- Ohio starts with 'State Procurement' and then 'Selling to the State'
- South Carolina actually lists on its official site, state agencies opportunities with the title 'Matching Grants'
- Texas has an elaborate site—start the search with 'State and Local Bid Opportunities' and then 'Texas Marketplace—Bid Opportunities'
- Utah's official site has 'Business Online Services' then 'State Government' followed by 'Current Bidding Opportunities'
- Vermont starts with 'Vermont Agencies and Departments' then click 'State Government' followed by clicking 'Bid Opportunities'
- Washington state begin with 'Doing Business in Washington' and then click 'Bidding Opportunities'

3

Key Elements Enhance Success

✦

Winning Aspects To Emphasize

Not all grant application submissions are persuasive to reviewers, nor are they all funded. Obviously, some grant applications are more successful than others. It is certainly important that the grant application be written as clear and succinctly as possible. Most granting agencies will be receiving more applications than they can possibly fund. Later in the book, there will be a detailed discussion about how to construct a winning grant proposal.

ELEMENTS OF SUCCESS

Fiscal Accountability
Unit Costs
Collaborations
View Criteria

Certain elements enhance success. One of these is **fiscal accountability**. Can your organization concretely demonstrate that it has in place the necessary fiscal accountability measures that will ensure that the granting agency's dollars will be spent exactly as specified in the grant application? The government does audit most organizations receiving government funding. Even governments are audited. For example, the federal government audits state governments to ensure that the money was spent as specified.

How can you demonstrate fiscal accountability? In some government applications there will be direct questions about this issue. Don't brush off these questions with a cursory answer. Provide as much detail as possible about how these government funds will be segregated from other funds the organization receives. It is of particular interest to government auditors, how an organization will track personnel costs identified in the grant application. An organization may be asked to supply pay stubs.

Do not apply for government grants if your organization does not use the services of an outside accounting firm to audit the organization's books. An independent audit is of the utmost importance.

Unit Costs

Think of the government funding agency as a smart shopper. The government reviewers are looking at unit costs. Government agency raters will be comparing how much product—services or outputs of some kind—can be produced among the competing applications. If your organization has the capacity to inexpensively deliver a particular program or service because it creatively uses volunteers or interns; then the organization should emphasize that fact in the grant application. Organizations where the personnel costs are high because of expansive benefits such as health insurance or retirement plans are at a disadvantage when it comes to unit cost comparisons unless they have some other factor that minimizes these high costs. However, this alone should not discourage potential grantees from applying since the delivery of high quality or innovative or highly effective programs is important to government reviewers. Cost is not the only factor.

Collaborations

Government granting agencies, in their cost cutting mind-sets, need to make every dollar count so collaborations become extremely important. Some grant applications will demand the existence and functioning of collaboration as an eligibility criterion. The eligibility criteria will spell out exactly the composition of the collaborators. For example, in a health-related research project the collaborations could be among a local government entity, a private or public institution of higher learning and some organization (most likely a non-profit) that can conduct effective community outreach. Usually these organizations don't exist so they need to be constructed for the purposes of the grant. By submitting the grant application to the granting agency certain demands must be met. Most commonly, the members of the collaboration must have written agreements spelling out the exact responsibilities of each member of the collaboration.

Individual—Fiscal Agent

Collaborations are often the best tool for individuals seeking to obtain grant funding. Most government granting agencies do not permit individuals to submit applications. However, a resourceful individual can work with a non-profit organization and either designate the non-profit organization as the fiscal agent, or simply work as a sub-contractor for the organization. For the non-profit this can be a low cost alternative to having or hiring specific staff for a project or program.

Criteria

Government grants are ordinarily reviewed by career civil servants based on written criteria located within the RFP or announcement. Information required in the grant application is often assigned specific points. The actual point system will change from grant to grant, agency to agency. However, the concept is universal. The government agency needs to have a reasonably objective and formal system in place. An actual rating sheet will be created for each applicant. Under the Freedom of Information Act the rating can be made available to the public. Often an applicant will be asked to send three, four, or perhaps even six copies, and this reflects the number of reviewers involved in the process.

Be sure to carefully read how the point system is allocated. For example, a recent Health & Human Services grant on Sexually Transmitted Diseases had only two categories: Plan Description (60 points) and Capacity (40 points). There were only a few questions pertaining to each of these statements in the Criteria section of the announcement. However, in the body of the RFP there were a series of far more detailed questions. It then becomes the challenge of the grant writer to incorporate into all the other discussion points these two major criteria described in the RFP.

It is quite common to have the RFP list five, six, or even more specific criteria. Typically, NIH lists five criteria: significance, approach, innovation, investigator and environment. Many NIH RFPs list the five criteria but don't specify a numerical point system. Instead, the RFP states that the reviewers will make the determination. However, the RFP will provide information on the expected "Objectives and Scope" of the proposed program/project. The areas of interest to NIH are provided in the RFP as examples of studies that are more likely to be funded.

The New York State RFP criteria for Early Childhood Development is a model design format. Each selection criteria is clearly listed (there are seven); and the issues to be addressed for each criteria are given. In addition, the point system is placed on the page next to each criterion that is listed so immediately the grant writer can determine where the reviewers are expecting the strengths of the submission to be placed. In the case of the Early Childhood Development programs, the greatest importance rests with budgetary issues.

When preparing drafts of the submission, keep reminding yourself which criteria the government reviewers are emphasizing. On the draft page write the points assigned to each criterion. Imagine that you are writing a critical essay and the professor assigns points to each portion of the essay. You can get partial credit for an answer.

It has also become far more common that RFPs will include several grant announcements. Unless the instructions state otherwise, an organization is free to apply to all the potential award categories. However, the criteria is often different for each grant category and for federal grant applications that means completely separate forms for each award category.

Don't Agree To More Than The Organization Can Handle

Never commit to more than your organization can complete during the grant period. This is a common mistake of organizations. If the RFP requires that an organization provide services for up to three distinct categories of populations such as minorities, women and geographic areas with high rates of a specific disease, don't automatically conclude that your organization must provide coverage for all three populations. If the RFP requires no more than three populations but it's acceptable to serve only one population go for less unless the organization is completely prepared to cover all three areas. There are no extra points by the reviewers if your plan is expansive, especially if the reviewers don't think the organization can deliver on its promises.

4

Judging the Future Based on Past Performance

◆

Making Effective Use of the Organization's History & Accomplishments

Why should a government granting agency trust your organization with public money? How is your organization structured and what has it accomplished in the past? These are questions that need to be addressed in any grant application. However, unlike many foundation grant applications, these questions are rarely addressed directly by a government grant application.

EMPHASIS
Organizational History
Past Accomplishments
Staff

These factors are important to weave into the basic narrative of the project. Government grant reviewers are not looking for Pulitzer prize winning narratives; yet the case must be made that your organization has the experience, the necessary staff and the capacity to achieve the goals and objectives written in the grant application. In the case of faith-based organizations, it is essential to demonstrate the religious mission of an organization and at the same time establish walls that separate religious worship from the ability to deliver services. If it can be done, introduce the organization's official mission statement into the narrative, especially if it incorporates a compelling reason for the existence of the organization.

Uniqueness

It is common for an agency to receive far more applications than it could possibly afford to fund. What's one way to present an appealing case? What about your organization is unique? Is it long-established? Is it the first in the neighborhood? Were the founders special in some measurable way? If the organization serves a special population: minorities, women, the disabled, or former prisoners; are members of these populations represented on the Board of Directors? Are staff also members of these special populations which the program/project is designed to serve? Does the organization follow a specialized training such as day care centers that utilize Montessori techniques or the center is a member of the National Association for the Education of Young Children (NAEYC)?

It's best to find something—anything that presents a uniqueness that separates your organization from the many others.

Past Accomplishments

The best proof of an organization's ability to succeed is to analyze what the organization has done in the past. Does the organization have an enviable track record? Can the reviewers pinpoint examples of past accomplishments that will lead them to expect similar results if they award a grant to the organization? Again, the grant application will probably not ask direct questions about past accomplishments, but it will indicate places where the information needs to be introduced.

The best method of demonstrating a track history is to build a story line. When did the organization start offering this service or a complimentary one? It is interesting to note if an organization started in a specific way and then proceeded to alter its course because of obstacles. This is a mark of a flexible and dynamic organization. No organization operates a program or service without problems.

If the organization offers a large number of different services its only necessary to provide a line or two about the services. The grant writer wants to focus on past accomplishments that prove or demonstrate that the organization is capable of meeting the announcement requirements. Do not fill up the pages with superfluous information. The reviewers do not have the time nor inclination to read pages of fluff. Focus on what the organization has done in the past that has a direct link to its ability to do something similar in the future.

If the organization has never done this specific service or program requested in the RFP, a different approach is necessary. Then the story line has to move in another direction. Why now is the organization capable of entering into a new service or program? Where specifically in its history are there similar links? Did the organization add new staff with a new set of expertise? Did the organization initiate new collaborations that allow it to enter into new territory? Did the community change and its needs shift? Is the organization moving with the community towards new programs and services?

The past accomplishments must be very specific. It's not enough to just indicate the organization did this or that. Give dates, places, numbers served. Does the organization have press stories that support its accomplishments? Don't send copies of the press reports; weave the information into the story line. Valuable attachments are letters of support from community leaders, other organizations, political figures that support past accomplishments and the potential of the organization to achieve the goals and objectives in the application. It is always easier to draft a letter of support to an organization or individual and then they can modify the letter in their own style.

If the organization has successfully received government grants then it's important for the new reviewers to know that information. The easiest way to display that information is through creating a simple table with the vital information such as grant title, amount, which government agency, short phrase on purpose, and dates.

Staff Distinctiveness

An organization's strength arises from its staff. The easiest way of demonstrating the organization can meets the goals and objectives of the grant application is through the utilization of specific staff. Many grant applications will request job descriptions and resumes to accompany the application. Those should be included whether or not they are requested as attachments. However, that's not enough. It is important to emphasize the skills, education, and experience of specific staff in the body of the grant submission. It should be emphasized that it's these skills that will make it possible for the organization to achieve the aims of the grant application. Not only are the past important accomplishments of the organization to be stated, but also the past achievements of specific staff. Do they have awards or press stories worthy of noting? Do particular staff members have interesting personal stories to repeat in the grant application as supportive documentation?

The tricky issue is when there is no specific staff in place. Organizations may wait until the funding is available before they go out and hire staff. If this is the case, then it is the job description that becomes important as demonstrating proof of potential new accomplishments.

Capacity to Meet Program/Project Goals and Objectives

This is the selling point. Will the organization be able to meet its obligations? What is there about this organization, as opposed to other organizations bidding for the dollars, that assures the reviewers the money will be well spent? There may be direct questions about this issue and the grant application must address them head on with specifics. The specifics include fiscal accountability, past accomplishments, service to the community, staff distinctiveness and measurable/reasonable goals and objectives.

Unlike most foundation or corporate grants, the government is rarely interested whether the project is sustainable after the funding period. Government funding is usually multi-year and so it is expected that the program or service will continue for the three or five years of the funding cycle. The government doesn't assume an organization will continue a program or service in the absence of continued government funding. In the rare instances that the question is asked, then the organization must address it. Usually questions of sustainability are directed at other levels of government and assume that local taxpayers will want to continue the program/service so fees will be established or a special tax levied.

There are exceptions to this rule. Government grant money that serves as seed money will have a strong emphasis on sustainability. For example, if the state government provides grant funds to create or expand a day care center or a charter school then it is expected that funding must be available after the initial period.

5

What's The Problem?

✦

Why Should This Project/Program be Funded

Unlike foundation or corporate grant applications where the problem may be quite vague, government grants usually address specific issues and problems. In the RFP description there may be pages of explanation why the government is interested in this problem. There is nothing to be gained by restating the obvious. However, a good grant application will succinctly describe how it is specifically addressing what may be a national or state problem.

Statement of Need

**PROBLEMS &
YOUR SOLUTIONS**

Statement of Need

Demographics – Pictures

Tell a Thousand Words

Competition – Think

Marketing

This section is the justification for why the project/program should be funded. It may or may not be directly addressed as a specific targeted part of the criteria; but regardless, it must be addressed. Here is where the grant applicant describes the community that will be served by the grant funding. The description of the problem must be very specific to the location chosen. Form 424 of the federal "Application For Federal Assistance" directly asks: 'Areas Affected by Project (Cities, Counties, States, etc).'

The grant application should identify physical, economic, social, financial, institutional or other problems that will be addressed by successful funding of the application. If possible create maps that pinpoint the actual geography. In the RFP the granting agency will discuss the purpose of the RFP, and within this description will be the key dimensions to emphasize in a statement of need section. For example, in a recent federal RFP on childhood obesity, the statement of the problem was clearly provided. "Research has shown that obesity in childhood tracks into adulthood, carrying along with it increased susceptibility to hypertension, dyslipidemia and glucose intolerance. In fact, the striking increase in the prevalence of childhood obesity over the past 30 years has been associated with a marked increase in the incidence of type 2 diabetes among adolescents."

So, the Statement of Need has to directly address two issues. First, demonstrate that the community has a problem by providing statistics concerning overweight children, adolescents with type 2 diabetes, adults with diabetes, etc. Also consider how the statistics have changed over the past ten or twenty years. Second, the program described in the application must be designed to meet this problem with specific interventions that are effective. Statistics should be included that identify successful interventions. If the program being considered in the grant application is entirely novel or innovative then there must be statistics to indicate positive change will occur. There must be hints or possibilities described in the literature that point in this direction. Using reputable references is important; actual citations from acceptable professional or scientific journals are encouraged.

Use of Demographics

Every grant application should contain some type of demographic information. The best comparisons are between the subject area and the larger community. For example, if the area under consideration is a zip code, compare this zip code with the city or county, the state and the nation if it makes the problem more pressing. Comparisons should always be included, but carefully choose which statistics make a better case. It isn't that statistics lie, but some present a more compelling story.

The most effective way of demonstrating the power of demographic analysis is graphically. It is a true adage that in using demographic information, "a picture is worth a thousand words." The easiest approach to effectively create graphs and tables for inclusion in the grant application is by using Microsoft's Excel software. It is easy to insert these tables and charts into the text if you're using Microsoft's Word software. There are many better, more sophisticated statistical packages that produce beautiful charts and tables, but for ease of use, Word combined with Excel software does a nice job. The writer doesn't need to have any real knowledge of statistics or demographics to use the Excel software.

The most common graphic charts in the Excel software are column, bar, line and pie. Personal choice can determine which type of graph or chart is used, but remember that reviewers will probably be seeing the application and its attachments in black and white. Applications are usually reproduced for reviewers on black and white printers or copiers.

The Excel software column graph selections include: cluster, stacked, 100% stacked and then 3D visual effects. Again, unless the intent is to include all copies with color graphs the 3D Versions can be distracting. The bar graphs are similar to column graphs except that the information is displayed horizontally rather than vertically. For information that looks at points over time such as monthly clinic visits over a year, daily arrests during the week, a line graph is a good pictorial choice. Using the line graph, Excel lets you then compare the geographic area under consideration for the grant with some other geography such as a city, county, state or the nation. A pie chart is also a favorite choice. It's usually easy to read and a means of displaying information in a highly descriptive manner. Practical examples of using pie charts are describing the ethnic/racial backgrounds of an area's population or results of a customer satisfaction question. The best looking pie charts use color so remember that fact in using them in a grant application. As always when working with any type of charts, never overwhelm the reader with too many categories. It's best to keep things simple.

Where To Go

Where does an organization find reliable demographic information on items such as age, race/ethnicity, income, poverty rates and gender? Begin with local government sources. Most cities and towns maintain some demographic information on their community for use by the local Planning and Zoning Board. All state agencies also maintain detailed information on the state either in the Planning Department or through the Economic Development Department.

The best single source of all demographic data is the US Bureau of the Census. The web site is www.census.gov. Look for the Census Bureau's "American Factfinder." After you locate that site, click on "Fact Sheet." This is a remarkable site for almost an unlimited amount of information on a large variety of demographic subjects such as population, housing, poverty, education, income, commuting to work, migration, etc. The problem is that it is not a particularly user friendly site. It takes experience to maneuver through the many sources of specific information.

Other great sources of demographic information vary depending on the source of the information. For example, the federal Department of Justice is the place to go for crime statistics. There is a sub-agency that collects data of all kinds. For medical and disease information the sources are The Centers for Disease Control (CDC) or National Institutes of Health (NIH).

Competitive Analysis—Who Else is Doing This

Although a RFP may never directly ask about whom else in the community is doing what your organization's grant application is proposing, inevitably this is an issue. Think of the grant application as a product which will be compared to other similar products in the marketplace. If you consider the application as a marketing tool for the project/program, then assume two forms of competition: other applicants and other existing organizations or programs in the community not requesting funding. There is a fear by government funders of encouraging unnecessary duplication of services.

As a part of the Statement of Need material include information about other programs or organizations that are doing similar activities in the community where the program is proposed. It is a rare event when there is nothing else around in the community. Should this actually be the case, then make certain that the uniqueness of the program itself is prominently discussed in the grant application. If there are programs in the community that appear similar, the grant application must concretely describe how the applicant's submission is somehow different and superior to what is already available. Emphasizing the improved nature of the program is key to effectively marketing the value of the organization's application.

Demonstration or Pilot Program

Requests for applications that specifically seek "demonstration" or "pilot programs" are truly gifts. Search out RFPs that have these twin words—demonstration project or pilot project in the titles. It usually means that the common way of dealing with this problem isn't working. The government has decided because a problem may be new or so long-entrenched that something totally innovative is needed. It is then the organization's challenge to show that it has the talents, experiences or expertise that lends itself to successfully diving into something new. An organization that has a reputation for successfully make changes in the community or solving intractable problems is a viable candidate for a successful award, even if it does not have a track record with the government itself.

6

The Body of the Grant Application

◆

Tell the Story Concisely but with a Compelling Message

CONTENTS

Program Narrative

Goals and Objectives

Speak to the Language of
the RFP/RFA

A government grant application consists of several parts and all of them are essential in order for the grant to be even considered by government reviewers. Think of the application as a book comprised of chapters. However, each chapter does not carry equal weight in a point system developed by the reviewers. Before diving into the application read and re-read the description that is the framework for the program narrative. Within the RFP, there is often a discussion of the problem or need—the reason for the RFP. The government has decided to fund the RFP because it has accumulated information that leads it to believe there is a problem that needs to be solved. The inclusion of government sources of information reflects the government's previous investment. It is recommended that an organization, even if it is familiar with the problem, search out those references and read them. Valuable information is usually contained in the sources. If the RFP provides direct web site linkages to source material then the reviewers expect applicants to be familiar with the source material. If possible use the source material in the program narrative. Inclusion of this material indicates that the applicant is familiar with the information. If possible refer to or directly quote the source material as a justification for the application submission and the organization's ability to be successful at tackling the problem.

Program Narrative

The Program Narrative is the backbone of an application submission. In many cases, the grant application will require the inclusion of a section labeled "Program Narrative." There is no standard template that an organization can use for this section. However, the rationale for the application submission is contained in this section.

Instructions

There are always instructions that accompany the Program Narrative section. Follow the instructions precisely. The instructions often require seemingly insignificant requisites but pay attention to all of them. Typically these instructions include: maximum length of the document, paging, font size, spacing and margins of each page, organization's name on each page or the opposite—no name on the pages. If the document is not sent electronically then there will be requirements about the number of copies as well as original signatures.

The page length requirement for the Program Narrative is a very important starting point. There are rarely a minimum number of pages required but often the maximum is clearly stated. The page length of the Narrative varies dramatically. (Applications can be as short as 10 pages or as long as 45 pages.)

As a rule, the Program Narrative section is open to the interpretation of the submitting applicant. There may be some big questions to be answered but unlike many foundation or corporate grants, it is unlikely that an applicant will complete a set of simple yes and no questions. The narrative is like a school paper—it is left to the imagination of the writer to describe the problem, specifically indicate how to solve it, and follow-up with a plan on how to evaluate the success of the venture.

Executive Summary

Sometimes the Program Narrative requires the inclusion of an Executive Summary, Program Summary or an Abstract. Write the summary last because then it will be easier to summarize the proposed program/project. The request for an Abstract may also include restrictions, usually it is framed as a summary description of 250 words or less. Use the 'Word Count' tool in Microsoft's Word software to ensure that the Abstract is the proper length.

The Executive Summary usually has restrictions. Typically, the summary should be one page in length or no more than two pages. As always with government restrictions, follow them precisely.

Key Sections

One can expect that the Program Narrative should contain information on the need for the program/project. However, there may be a distinct and separate section called 'Statement of Need'. Then there is the marketing of the organization; why your organization is the perfect instrument for solving the problem. This is usually followed by a detailed discussion of the goals and objectives and the specific actions the organization will undertake to implement the goals and objectives.

Usually a Program Narrative will also require a detailed 'Evaluation Plan'. It is often viewed more favorably if the evaluation plan is actually conducted by an outside organization or individual. In some RFPs this will be a specific requirement. In the budget, provide funds for the development and completion of an evaluation plan. If the organization does not have the expertise to write a grant application, and is so cash strapped that it is unable to pay for the services of an outside grant writer, you may be able to actually fund the grants writer through providing funding through the evaluation plan. In many instances an effective grants writer can also serve as the evaluator.

A Program Narrative may require a 'Management Plan'. Here it is important to highlight the specific talents, experiences and expertise of all the individuals involved in the program/project. The Management Plan may require providing organization charts with designated lines of authority.

Also, Program Narratives can have quirky requirements. One may require a 'Table of Contents' especially if the narrative is lengthy—45 pages. Others require the completion and inclusion of special tables and charts. Some narratives permit the grant writer to reconstruct a table or chart to make it easier to complete if there isn't any way to electronically access the table. However, some grant applications, particularly with state agencies, you must complete and submit the actual table included in the grant application materials neither a copy or a computer-generated facsimile is acceptable.

Prepare an Outline

This is a suggestion, particularly for an organization that has never previously applied to the government. Start by reading and diagramming the essential points described in the Purpose of the Public Announcement or RFP. The RFP may identify specific objectives that the government is seeking. These objectives must be addressed in the grant submission and presumably the application's Program Narrative will describe how the organization plans on solving or minimizing the problem. Some government agencies are renowned for their problem solving abilities. For example, because The National Institutes of Health conducts and funds a wide range of research, it expects the applicant to build on the existing body of knowledge. The outline can assist the writer in determining where to insert outside information or demographic tables as well as what materials should be included in constructing a successful application.

The outline is a guide in constructing the winning and compelling story about the program/project. It need not be elaborate but it should assist the grant writer in the construction of the Program Narrative.

Some grant submissions require the completion and inclusion of a "Checklist" while others simply include a checklist as a guide to the grant writer. If a checklist doesn't exist among the application materials, create one to use with the outline.

Goals and Objectives

This section is often hastily constructed resulting in the program/project being rejected. Consider this section as an evaluation tool, which reviewers go through and determine whether the program/project is feasible. The goals and/or objectives (each agency uses different language) are essentially the plan on how the organization intends to meet the problem addressed earlier in the Program Narrative.

If the information in the Announcement speaks to the government having specific goals and objectives, such as reducing minority infant mortality or violent crime, then the grant submission should include addressing the funders' goals. Often in the referenced information in the Announcement section of the RFP, the sources cited are government reports that mention overall goals and objectives. If you can incorporate these government goals and objectives into the program/project being proposed then it demonstrates the organization's familiarity with the problem.

The RFP expects that the goals and objectives are measurable and can be completed in specific time frames. This information must be included in a Goals and Objectives section, or somewhere else in the Program Narrative. Sometimes the RFP will suggest or require that this information be detailed in a table format. If possible, even if not requested, construct the goals and objectives in an easy to read table. This will force the grant writer to test the logic of the goals and objectives as well as the actions to be taken. Staring at all the vital information in a table format makes it easier to notice timing issues or the sequence of events.

A model table can be constructed that lists each goal or objective, followed by specific actions that will be taken, when these actions will occur, which individuals will be responsible or involved in the actions, how it will be measured and how it will be evaluated. The time table can be either in months or quarters depending on the nature of the grant submission.

Speak to the Language of the RFP/RFA

Use the jargon that is cited in the RFP/RFA. Each government agency has its own specific language and these words need to be repeated in the grant submission. The government is famous for its use of acronyms and assumes that anyone responding to a RFP will be familiar with its use of language. Acronyms and jargon are just shorthand and if you want to join the club then it is expected you are well versed in the language.

Again, if government sources are cited in the RFP, read them and use them in the grant submission. Use information from government sites in developing the goals and objectives section as your organization's plan to further the government's goal to reduce a problem or change a situation or create a new environment. In creating the Program Narrative also consider the reviewers stated Criteria in the RFP.

The trick of developing an effective grant application in response to a RFP is thinking like a government reviewer. How would you rate the application? Essentially, the grant writer is weaving a good story, using the language of the RFP, reinforcing the government's efforts in the area and gaining the most points by effectively building on the criteria enumerated in the RFP/RFA. It is often helpful to have an outside person read the grant submission to ensure it is building an effective story and the flow is logical.

7

Writing the Budget

♦

Does the Organization have a feasible financial plan?

Nothing is more important than a carefully constructed budget based on realistic numbers and a justification for all the dollars requested. The federal application process usually requires that specific forms be completed and submitted with the grant submission. Form 424A—'Budget Information—Non-Construction Programs' is a two page form that is not difficult to complete. However, the tough part is carefully crafting a budget that passes the federal reviewers' feasibility analysis. Has the organization created a budget that reflects the costs of developing a program/project and will the award amount permit the successful implementation of the goals and objectives described in the Program Narrative? Instructions for the SF (Standard Form) 424A are provided on-line. The Form 424A is designed to accommodate requesting funding from one or more government grant sources. If an organization is developing a program/project that is requesting funding from a variety of federal government sources, the entire request can be listed on one form.

BUDGETING

Personnel Services

Indirect Charges

In-kind or matching

Requirements

Restrictions

The budget categories or 'object class categories' are listed on the Form 424A. They are ordinary categories one would use in any budget: personnel, fringe benefits, travel, equipment, supplies, contractual, construction, other. This particular form 424A includes a category labeled construction but it is to be used when the applicant is not requesting federal government funding for construction purposes. If construction is required but will be paid by other than non-federal government funding it is to be listed on Form 424A. In the case where the applicant is seeking federal government funding for construction purposes use Form 424C 'Budget Information—Construction Programs.'

In developing a budget, the two major categories are personnel costs (in many cases the majority of the expenses) and OTPS—Other than Personnel Services. This budget form does not separate the costs in the customary fashion. It is a simpler form because each category gets its own individual listing. What is most important for federal government reviewers is how the program will be funded. Does the applicant intend to use other sources of funding including program income—revenue?

It also requires that the program budget be allocated by quarters. The easiest method is to simply divide the requested funding by four. However, that approach may not be the most appropriate based on how costs are expected to be spent. Whether or not the budget receives high points as one of the selection criteria, government reviewers will carefully scrutinize the budget. Do not be misled by the simple forms, the budget is one of the most important pieces of the grant submission.

As of 2005, if the organization is receiving $500,000 or more annually from the federal government, then the organization must prepare and submit the infamous A-133 Audit. This is an expensive audit that must be prepared by a highly competent, outside auditing firm familiar with the rules and regulations concerning the A-133 Audit. It is reasonable to expect that the cost of such an audit can range from $20,000-$25,000. The dollar amount triggering an A-133 Audit has been rising; it was $300,000 in 2004. That dollar amount is based on totaling all federal government awards for the year so that two awards of $250,000 apiece will trigger the A-133 Audit.

Personnel Services

This is the key component of the budget. It is an unusual grant application that does not include personnel expenses. Without adequate funding for personnel the program/project cannot move forward. The federal Form 424A does not require many details on the form itself; however, the budget narrative that must accompany the form will require details. A typical federal submission will require a detailed 12 month budget, and a less specific budget for the entire proposed project period. Typically, a federal government grant is three to five years in duration. State grant budget submissions often require the completion of multiple forms requiring great specificity about the use of the requested funds. The possible logic is that state awards are to smaller and less sophisticated organizations, so the budget reviewers require more demands regarding specificity to ensure the appropriate use of the funding.

In constructing the project/program budget start with the direct personnel responsible should the organization receive funding. If there is an incumbent in the position, typically a federal or state application will require a biographic sketch. Regardless, every grant submission should include a job description for each position. In developing the budget, think in terms of position title, percentage of time each position will dedicate to the program/project based on a 12 month period, and the salary/fringe benefits for each position. Then consider how the position will be funded—what sources will the organization be tapping to cover the costs of each position. For example, the position of Program Coordinator (title), will be dedicated to the project 100% of the time for 12 months. Now will the Program Coordinator position be funded 100% from this grant submission? Or will the position require funding from other sources such as program revenue, other federal or state funds, or fundraising sources? **WARNING:** If the organization intends to fund a position from more than one government source be warned that decision will raise a red flag for government fiscal reviewers. Government auditors are concerned with the issue of supplanting of government funds. What that means is the government thinks an organization is double dipping, paying for the same position twice from two separate government sources.

It is obvious that if an organization uses government funds, all expenditures must be carefully recorded; recordkeeping must be of the highest quality. Sometimes an organization provides documentation for each piece of equipment purchased and all printing and mailing, but then fails to maintain adequate personnel records. Be certain that personnel pay stubs are kept and clearly indicate the position's time spent on a government funded program/project.

Indirect Costs

Every government grant application is different regarding the acceptability of including indirect costs in the budget. The finance people in the organization will appreciate the value of using indirect costs, but in preparing the budget, read all the fine print concerning this issue. Being able to include this in a grant is considered a gift by most finance people, since it can cover general administrative costs seldom directly funded such as the accounting or legal staff, rental space, utilities and telephone.

If an organization is receiving, or actively seeking government funding for a variety of programs/projects the finance staff should consider negotiating with the government an acceptable, indirect rate. The advantage of such an agreed upon rate is that if the grant submission permits it, the organization simply plugs in the rate. However, if the rate is low then it may not be advisable to always use the same rate for each program/project. This is something the grant writer and the financial staff should discuss.

Also, the indirect cost is usually based on a specific percentage, but with strings attached. For example, the grant may state within the budgetary description in the RFP/RFA that an applicant can use an indirect expense of 10 percent. The 10% refers to expenses that have been approved by the government grant fiscal staff. So an organization may assume that a grant of $100,000 with an indirect cost of 10% automatically means there is $10,000 to offset the costs of the accounting and legal staff of the organization. This is not necessarily so, because the remaining $90,000 must be approved expenses. If the organization purchases a piece of equipment for $5,000 but the government agency fiscal staff rejects that expense (and this can happen), the indirect will be based on $95,000– $9,500 unless you can find a $5,000 cost that is acceptable to the government fiscal staff. **WARNING**—Even if the grant award budget lists equipment or supplies, do not spend the money until the organization receives specific, written approval for those items. The most common problem occurs over personnel expenses. An individual may leave the organization and there is a vacancy, and subsequently savings in the grant award. Get permission to redirect the personnel money to another purpose before moving forward and spending the money. That can also mean getting permission to pay the salary and fringe benefits of a new hire or a transfer within the organization.

In-kind Costs/Matching Requirements

The mandated inclusion of a matching funds requirement can be a deciding factor in whether to go forward and submit a grant application. A smaller organization should read the RFP/RFA carefully regarding this issue before moving ahead. Talk with the finance staff. If there is a matching requirement, the fiscal staff needs to carefully examine what types of indirect costs will satisfy the matching requirements.

In some cases, a federal government award cannot be matched by another federal government grant or any federal funds, while in other cases there are no restrictions. The tricky part about using other government funds for matching purposes is knowing exactly the source of that funding. For example, state government grant awards are often based on awards from the federal government. If there is restriction on the use of federal funding for matching purposes then check carefully the source of any state or local money. Although the award letter comes from the state or local government award, it may still be unacceptable. The best source of advice for these technical matters is the contacts that are listed in the RFP/RFA.

An organization can expect that if the RFP/RFA speaks about challenge grants, then matching will be required. A challenge grant can be challenging. The issue is usually that the amount of money the organization has to match grows while the federal contribution declines. Many foundation and corporate grants employ this type of matching requirement. The purpose in these changing financial requirements is to make the program/project self-sufficient because by design there are potential revenue streams or other fundraising possible. Ordinarily the match must also be new money and not in-kind.

Restrictions

There are rarely government grants without restrictions. There are two types of restrictions that require careful review by an organization. First, restrictions on activities the RFP/RFA will fund. These types of restrictions can be activities such as training when the RFP/RFA speaks about implementation. If the grant is successfully awarded, it may be that costs associated with training will be rejected. Second, there are usually restrictions on fundable expenditures. Every grant will be different but almost all have some type of budget restrictions. Carefully read what the grant will **NOT** pay for in the RFP/RFA. The usual "no-no's" are expenses linked to items such as travel. So the federal government will not pay for first class airplane travel. The government has an acceptable vehicle reimbursement rate and accepts no other rate. The restrictions can be much more formidable. If there is a question, discuss the issue with the government contact person. There are usually two different types of contacts listed in the RFP/RFA; a program contact and a fiscal contact. These people should become your new best friends.

Individuals are commonly excluded from directly receiving grant funding. In Chapter 9 "Individuals Need to be Creative", individual funding opportunities will be discussed. However, that restriction can be ameliorated by honest ingenuity. In some cases the restriction is openly discussed in the RFP/RFA by indicating that a nonprofit organization can function as a fiscal agent for an individual. In other cases using the fiscal agent concept, the individual is hired as a consultant for the program/project.

8

Rejection

✦

The rejection letter is only the beginning

The government actually appreciates an organization that is willing to try more than once. No is never the end of the discussion. In some cases, the government reviewers will include a letter detailing the shortcomings of a grant application. If a letter does not provide any specific reasons for the denial, there is nothing lost by making a call or sending an e-mail to one of the RFP/RFA contacts listed. No one may be willing to talk on the record, but it is worth the effort.

REJECTION LETTER

No is a New Beginning

Try Again

Who were the Winners

Study the Winners

A denial letter can provide the basis for the next application cycle. The organization's first effort may not have secured enough points. An organization can ask how many points it earned from the reviewers. While we would like to think that if we wrote a more compelling story the grant would have been funded, rarely is it that simple. Most of the time, the rejection has to do with the implementation plan (carrying out the goals and objectives) or the budget. The reviewers did not have faith that the information provided in the grant application was sufficient to assure that the plan would be carried out in a timely fashion. In some cases, the plan was simply not what the reviewers were looking for in an application. The plan was outside the parameters described in the RFP/RFA "Program" discussion. Although the RFP/RFA can speak to issues that are innovative or cutting edge, except in basic scientific research, it is probably not a great idea to introduce something totally outside the prevailing literature. Other typical shortcomings have to do with budgetary concerns or the expertise/experience of staff.

Consider the denial letter as a first step in the re-application process. Since most government grant cycles are similar year after year, start thinking ahead to the next deadline. If the government reviewers will not provide assistance ask another third party to review the grant application. Don't start rewriting the application, because it does happen that the next series of RFP/RFAs may have new selection criteria or a new point system. However, the organization has now gained the experience of applying and should have learned some things about the process or enough of it. A common problem is the failure to secure the appropriate outside support, if a partnership or coalition was required. This is the time to continue working on creating a more viable group.

The government reviewers look kindly on repeat applications. Now the organization has an easier time completing all the application forms. If the budget changes and the unit costs decline that is a good step. The organization's staff may have a track record of similar accomplishments to be better judged by the reviewers. The panel of government reviewers may remain the same individuals for the next round of reviews so a repeat application will be remembered. Also, there may be a question whether the organization has applied for this RFP/RFA in the past. If the new application is a much improved version from the prior submission than it should be prominently noted and the reasons for the changes skillfully introduced into the Program Narrative.

In many instances, past recipients of government funding are listed. There may be a useful description of the winning grant applications. Carefully examine the posted materials. Look for similar programs/projects but also the geographic distribution of the winning grant applications. The government has a certain obligation to spread around the wealth. If there are no winning applications from your community it can work in your organization's favor. The government reviewers probably don't want to neglect a particular area too many times. At the same time, if the community has a very successful model in place there may be no point in re-applying.

It isn't until an organization actually competes for government funding through the RFP/RFA process that it can truly appreciate the winners. As always with government funding, never discount the power of politics. For that reason, it is highly recommended (see Chapter 1) to have contacts in the offices of local, state and federal representatives.

9

Individuals need to be Creative

✦

Think Collaborations

Grant Funding for Individuals

There are two general categories of individuals likely to be awarded a direct government grant—artists and scholars/researchers. The grant awards can cover a variety of purposes. The grant award can be directly linked to the individual's implementation of a program or project. A grant award can also be a recognition of a lifetime of individual achievement. Some grant awards are geared to specific time frames such as promising young scholars (under 35 years of age) or scholars in their tenth year of professional work. Then there are highly competitive fellowships. A surprisingly wide variety of government agencies offer fellowships. The duration of the fellowship, the amounts of the award and restrictions on funding also vary.

The other common government funding available to individuals is internships. All levels of government offer internships to students from high school students to post graduates. A typical internship is for the summer; however, longer lengths of one year to multiple years are available.

The easiest path for an individual artist to follow is to receive government grant funding by working in association with a school, school district, college or the educational department of an arts/cultural organization. Most museums, orchestras, theatre groups even libraries operate educational programs for children, adults, seniors and special populations such as the disabled, minorities/disadvantaged, and/or immigrants. It is not an accident that visual artists, performers, writers and poets often teach to support their artistic endeavors. Government granting agencies are interested in projects/programs that enhance the learning experience of public school students, including those enrolled in charter schools, in grades K-12.

Scholars and researchers have a large range of federal agencies to explore for fellowships. The key is determining the most appropriate educational category. The individual can be an undergraduate college student, graduate school or post graduate Ph.D. The categories can be highly specific. For example, the individual researcher must have received their Ph.D. within the last five years.

The available research fellowships include practically all academic subjects. The research can be mundane. An example of a fellowship is one designed to improve the teaching of foreign languages among high school students. The subject matter can also be esoteric such as exploring potential unconventional advances in medicine or physics.

The number of direct awards to individuals is limited. Success is far more likely if the individual can link or coordinate or collaborate on his/her idea, project or program with an existing non-profit organization or educational institution. The only variable preventing an individual from receiving government grant funding is a lack of imagination and creativity on the part of the grant applicants.

Federal Agencies

The individual artist or scholar/researcher should regularly check on certain federal agency sites for new grant opportunities. Although it may not seem apparent but a wide range of federal agencies make grant opportunities available through fellowship programs.

What follows is a brief description of some selected federal agencies that offer fellowship opportunities. Some of these opportunities require that the applicant be a non-profit organization.

US Department of Justice

There are two programs that scholars with an interest in criminal justice should regularly check at the Department of Justice, Office of Justice Programs, National Institute of Justice www.ojp.usdog.gov/nij. One is the W.E.B. DuBois Fellowship Program and the other is the Graduate Research Fellowships. The DuBois Fellowship seeks fellows to focus on crime, violence, and the administration of justice in diverse cultural contexts. It also requires fellows to spend at least a minimum of 2 months at NIJ, which is located in Washington D.C.

The Graduate Research Fellowships program seeks students at the dissertation stage. It is assumed that the research subsidized by NIJ will lead to a Ph.D. and that the candidate's dissertation committee is fully supportive of the research. The official applicant for these fellowships is the sponsoring academic institution. This is typical of government fellowships. While the financial support is for the individual's expenses, the actual applicant is an academic institution. This is beneficial for the individual because it places the burden of financial accountability on an organization accustomed to meeting financial reporting demands.

US Department of Energy

The federal government is highly supportive of research endeavors that increase opportunities for junior academic faculty. The Department of Energy through its Office of Science has funding opportunities for junior faculty in widely diverse subjects. Again the applicant is the academic institution and in this case the supported investigator is a tenure-track physicist.

US Department of Defense

The Department of Defense through its US Army Medical Research and Materiel command operates the Idea Development Award. Independent investigators at all levels are eligible to submit proposals focused on innovative research. The individual conducts the research through an academic institution or research-oriented non-profit organization; and matching is expected from that organization or institution.

National Science Foundation

The National Science Foundation lists 21 pages of grant opportunities. Clearly, most are not designed for individuals but included are a variety of Fellowships. The best place to start is with NSF's Web site: www.nsf.gov and click under the heading, "Funding Opportunities."

The Graduate Research Fellowship Program (GRFP) sponsored by NSF lists opportunities in nine general academic categories including life sciences, chemistry, computer and information science and engineering, etc. Each fellowship subject category has similar application procedures but different deadlines. These broad categories cover the vast majority of all academic subjects. The caveats for these fellowships are four: 1) fellowships are awarded only for study leading to research-based master's or doctoral degrees; 2) research with disease-related goals is not eligible for support by NSF; 3) clinical and counseling psychology are generally not supported by this program; and 4) the research must include a scientific approach.

In addition, the NSF sponsors other fellowships or research opportunities. The following are just samples of what is available: International Research Fellowship Program, Louis Stokes Alliances for Minority Participation Program, Discovery Corps Fellowships; NSF Directors Award for Distinguished Teaching Scholars, Research Experiences for Undergraduate, GK-12:NSF Graduate Teaching Fellows in K-12 Education. Again the best advice is to check the NSF Web site.

National Endowment for the Arts

The National Endowment for the Arts is the largest annual funder for the arts in the United States. Congress appropriates its funding, which fluctuates with the political currents. Usually there is funding in the $100 million range. NEA then turns around and funds all the states. The result is that overall government (state and federal) funding for the arts is approximately $800 million annually. NEA funds a wide range of organizational and individual grants to all types of artists both established and unknown. In the past, it was a much more generous donor of grants to individuals, but as its money has been restricted, the agency's ability to fund individual artists has been cut. It was once the grantor for highly controversial artists, but that has also changed.

By 2005, the individual award categories had shrunk to literature fellowships and Jazz and Heritage lifetime awards. However, an individual artist should not be discouraged because there are still many opportunities to work through nonprofit organizations or educational institutions to receive government funding. NEA funds small agencies and the major arts organizations in the country. NEA awards grants in several categories: dance, design, folk and traditional arts, literature, media arts, music, musical theater, opera, theatre and visual arts in addition to museums, presenting (concert series), multidisciplinary and local arts agencies (other than state agencies).

NEA Literature Fellowships consist of two types: literature and translation projects. The two types of literature funded are prose and poetry. In alternating years either fiction or creative nonfiction is funded and then the next year poetry is funded. The FY 2008 federal application deadline is for prose fellowships (March 1, 2007) and FY 2007 (March 1, 2006) will be for poetry. Approximately forty literature fellowships are awarded annually; each award is $20,000. The translation projects are for the translation of prose, poetry or drama from any other language into English. This is awarded every year. This award is not designed for scholarly writing.

NEA Jazz Masters Fellowship awards are $25,000 and it is anticipated that 6 awards will be funded. The selection criteria are the excellence and significance of the nominee's contributions to the development and performance of jazz. There are five categories that are awarded, at least one award per category: rhythm instrumentalist, pianist, solo instrumentalist, vocalist and an arranger or composer. The funding is awarded through a nomination process and you cannot nominate yourself, someone else must do it.

NEA National Heritage Fellowship awards are $20,000 and ten are awarded each year. The awards are meant for master folk and traditional artists. The grant funding is also awarded through a nomination process and the individual must be nominated by another person or organization.

National Endowment for the Humanities

The National Endowment for the Humanities is a federal agency which funds grants that enhances and expands on the study of the humanities. The term humanities refers to language, (both modern and classical); linguistics; literature; jurisprudence; philosophy; archaeology; comparative religion; ethics; the history, criticism and theory of the arts; those aspects of social sciences which have humanistic content and employ humanistic methods; and the study and application of the humanities to the human environment with particular attention to reflecting on our diverse heritage, traditions and history.

Individuals may receive fellowship support through NEH. A full-time NEH fellowship is between 9-12 months and carries a stipend of $40,000. Fellowships are typically funded through colleges and universities but there are independent scholars who receive support. The application must be sent to NEH through the internet and applications are accepted between March 1 and May 1.

In addition to the fellowships, NEH awards summer stipends to scholars. The stipend is for two months of research and writing resulting in the publication of a scholarly article, monograph, book, archaeological site report, translations, or other scholarly activity. Again, typically the scholar receives funding through a college or university. The summer stipends are also on-line applications and the application deadline is between August 1 and October 1.

Although the subjects of the grant awards are in the realm of the humanities, the medium used can also be radio or television. Individuals working through a non-profit can apply for what NEH labels: Radio Projects: Consultation Grants; Radio Projects: Development and Production Grants; Television Projects: Consultation Grants; and Television Projects: Planning, Scripting or Production Grants.

10

Small Towns and Cities

✦

Awards to Smaller Political Jurisdictions

Special Funding Opportunities

The federal and state governments have created special programs just for small cities and towns. These grant opportunities are for all types of political divisions surrounding major cities, in the suburbs and in rural places. The definition of a small town and city is usually defined by population size although other types of designations are possible. Not every federal agency makes funding available to small cities and towns but many agencies do, including some of the largest such as Health and Human Services, Housing and Urban Development.

A selected group of grant opportunities is described below.

Historic Preservation

Small cities and towns seeking grant opportunities will find government funding for historic preservation available on both the federal and state level. A federal agency to consider is the National Park Service. The NPS offers funding through five general categories: American Battlefields, Historic Buildings, Historic Landmarks, Historic Landscapes and Tribal Communities. In addition to grant opportunities, the NPS publishes a series of publications (latest count 42 separate books) on topics related to historic preservation. For example, the TPS (Technical Preservation Services) Publications Catalog is available by calling 1-866-512-1800. Topics include "Assessing Cleaning and Water-Repellent Treatments for Historic Masonry Buildings," Exterior Pain Problems on Historic Woodwork," "The Preservation of Historic Barns," "Removing Graffiti from Historic Masonry."

The American Battlefield Protection Program (ABPP) promotes the preservation of significant historic battlefields and encourages states and small towns and cities to work with non-profit organizations and individual citizens to develop "planning and partnerships" for the protection of battle sites that currently cannot or should not be preserved in whole or in part by public ownership. The ABPP awards small matching funds (an average of $22,000) for sponsoring planning and education projects at historic battlefields.

The National Historic Landmarks Program can assist small cities and towns in obtaining this designation. The types of buildings that can be designated are quite varied and include the homes of famous people. For example, in 2004 the writer Eudora Welty's house in Jackson, Mississippi received the designation. Other popular landmarks are churches such as the recently designated First Unitarian Society Meeting House in Shorewood Hills, Wisconsin. Historic military complexes are also common places for designations such as Fort King located in Ocala, Florida and Camp Pine Knot in Hamilton County, New York. Federal designation of a building or site then makes it possible to receive other federal and state funding for renovations. The e-mail address for more information is: nps_hps-info@nps.gov. States provide funding to small cities and towns through the NPS Certified Local Government Program which is a matching grant program for the expansion and maintenance of the National Register of Historic Places and support of historic preservation activities. Another NPS funded program run by the states (usually a state Office of Parks & Recreation or Office of Historic Preservation) is the Land and Water Conservation Fund Program. This program specifically provides matching funds for the acquisition, development and/or rehabilitation of outdoor park and recreation facilities. Other federal agencies work with the states to operate funding programs such as the Federal Highway Administration's Land and Recreational Trails Program. This state-run, federally funded program provides matching grants to small cities and towns for the acquisition, development, rehabilitation and maintenance of trails and trail-related projects.

Environmental Programs

One of the most important federal agencies involved with environmental issues is the US Environmental Protection Agency www.epa.gov. This is the agency that provides funding for brownfields site clean-ups, prevention, assessment and sustainable reuse. In particular, the EPA is interested in providing financial assistance to small cities or towns where the brownfields cleanup is in low-income and socio-economically disadvantaged communities. Brownfield sites are defined by EPA as one contaminated by petroleum or a petroleum product, controlled substances and mine-scarred lands. EPA offers grants for training, research and technical assistance as well as job training grants. A typical assessment grant is for up to $200,000 to assess a site for contamination by hazardous substances, pollutants or contaminants. The Revolving Loan Fund (RLF) grant may be initially awarded up to $1 million. A Cleanup grant is usually no more than $200,000 per site for cleanup. A small city or town can use up to 10% of its grant funds for monitoring the health of local populations exposed to one or more hazardous substances, pollutants or contaminants from a brownfield site.

States such as New York operate extensive brownfield programs designed to aid local communities. For example New York State's Municipal Assistance for Environmental Restoration Projects is designed to spur the cleanup and redevelopment of brownfields. The state will provide up to 90 % of on-site eligible costs and 100% of off-site eligible costs for site investigation and remediation activities. Once remediated, the property may then be reused for commercial, industrial, residential or public use. The guidelines require that the municipality must own the property and cannot be responsible for the contamination. Investigation grants are to determine the nature and extent of the contamination and the appropriate remedy. The investigation must include public input on the selection of the cleanup remedy and ends with a Record of Decision (ROD). Remediation grants include the design and construction of the cleanup selected in the ROD. The web site is: www.dec.state.ny.us/website/der/erp/. Another NYS program of interest to small cities and towns is the Brownfield Opportunity Area Program which is designed to provide technical and financial assistance to conduct redevelopment planning for designed areas containing brownfield sites.

The state of New Jersey runs the Site Remediation Program and money is available through the Hazardous Discharge Site Remediation Fund (www.nj.gov/dep/srp/brownfields/process.htm. Small cities or towns that own contaminated sites are eligible. Grants and low interest loans are available for various remedial activities. Small cities and towns may apply for amounts up to $2 million per year for investigation and cleanup activities. Once a preliminary assessment, site investigation or remedial investigation has proceeded, then you may apply for cleanup funds through low interest loans up to $2 million per year.

New England is home to many old manufacturing sites that are currently vacant because of environmental contamination. Different states have different approaches to encourage new industrial, commercial or residential development on these sites. For example, Connecticut makes most of its brownfields money available directly to developers. Small amounts are available to small cities or towns to conduct Phase I (up to $3,000) and Phase II (up to $10,000) to conduct assessments and investigations. The Connecticut Brownfields Redevelopment Authority is the responsible agency: www.ctbrownfields.com/grants_redevelopment.

The state of Rhode Island operates its brownfields program through the state Economic Development Corporation. The RIEDC receives money from the federal EPA and disperses it to small cities and towns to conduct site investigations. In addition, the Rhode Island Department of Environmental Management (RIDEM) operates the EPA Brownfields Cleanup Revolving Loan Fund that awards low interest loans for the cleanup of brownfields: www.riedc.shazamm.net/riedc.

Other states run similar programs. In fact, most states have funding for environmental clean-ups because the states receive funding from the federal government. For more information check with an official state web site for the state agency(ies) involved in environmental issues such as a state Environmental Protection Agency or Economic Development Department.

Main Street Programs

It has become apparent with population shifts and the introduction of gigantic shopping malls and large mega stores such as Wal-Mart and Home Depot that the downtowns of many small cities and towns have been declining. The purpose of the Main Street programs across the country has been the revitalization of downtown districts. Successful Main Street programs have lead to greater economic development opportunities for those selected communities. The downtowns look nicer, enhancing the image, leading to more people visiting and shopping in the area.

There is a four point approach taken by the Main Street Programs. It starts with **Organization**. A local Main Street group or committee is created that includes local businesses, residents, civic groups, bankers, public officials and the Chamber of Commerce. The foundation of the Main Street Program is that this is a long-term effort fueled by volunteers dedicated to downtown revitalization. For this to work those individuals who volunteer are committed stakeholders in the future of the downtown district because revitalization doesn't happen overnight. The second component is **Promotion**—marketing the downtown as a viable and enjoyable shopping and visiting experience. Image becomes an important ingredient in success. The third component is **Economic Restructuring** by changing the mix of downtown businesses to more accurately reflect residents' tastes and shopping needs. It can also mean changing zoning regulations to convert unused space into new uses. The fourth and most obvious component is **Design**. How can the committee enhance the visual appeal, attractiveness and sometimes the traffic flow within the downtown district? Design elements include the simplest such as cleaning up the streets and alleys. Making a downtown district look orderly, repairing broken sidewalks, installing new landscaping and street banners, upgrading street lighting can all significantly enhance the physical characteristics of the downtown district, and therefore encourage more consumer traffic.

Not every state has a Main Street Program. Six states do not participate including New York, Montana, Alaska, Idaho, Nevada and Wyoming. To check on opportunities in New Jersey see the website: www.state.nj.us/dca/dhcr/msnj.shtml. Connecticut's program is run through a non-profit organization working with major corporations such as Connecticut Light and Power Company. See website www.ctmainstreet.org. Rhode Island has three funded programs in Gloucester, South Kingstown and Warren.

For other state programs, check with the official state web site and inquire about the Main Street Program.

11

In Conclusion

◆

Awards Keep Coming Even in Tough Economic Times

Good luck with writing your grant proposal. There are opportunities out there for groups of all kinds as well as individuals. Do not get discouraged if your proposal is rejected; remember the advice from the first line of this book. The United States government has billions of dollars earmarked for grants. With determination and a well organized proposal, your grant proposal can succeed.

Under the current federal government economic climate one might assume that grants will become more difficult to obtain. Actually, what does happen is that federal priorities shift so that grant opportunities do not disappear but changes are likely. Although the federal government's new priorities may be different and not adequate for meeting the funding needs of every organization, state government funding opportunities can substitute in areas once dominated by the federal government. Despite pressures on the federal treasury, many state government are flush with cash which they will make available for new programs and projects.

The best approach is to design a funding strategy that looks at the many varied potential sources of funding that an organization or even an individual can successfully obtain. This comprehensive strategy requires understanding that funding must be diverse especially if it's directed at a specific proposal or program. The following are only suggestions:

- Federal Government
- State Government
- City/County/Local Government

- Private Foundations
- Family Foundations
- Individual Donations/Sponsors
- Revenues—Bidding for Contracts

Searching for government support is more an art than a science, look everywhere and it is okay if you use a wide range of sources sometimes resulting in receiving duplicate announcements. While the internet is becoming the tool to use for researching where to find grants, unfortunately, it is still in its formative stage. The federal government is becoming more of a master in using new technology to communicate with would-be applicants, but state and local governments are lagging.

One logistical problem is that someone has to review all the announcements and information that is received. A knowledgeable person must read through the materials to determine whether the grant announcement is something worth pursuing. The place to start the reviewing process is with the eligibility category. By evaluating that category first, one can establish immediately if the applicant can be a non-profit, a city, faith-based organization, an individual or a for-profit organization.

Use this book as a resource while researching and writing a proposal. We live in a fast paced world so be prepared and nimble as you cast out a net for potential sources of government funding.

978-0-595-37785-5
0-595-37785-8